Over 9,200 cursive tracing units!

Beginning Cursive

Alphabet Handwriting Practice

- Uppercase Cursive Letters

- Lowercase Cursive Letters

- Cursive Sentence Practice

"Learning to write in cursive is shown to improve brain development in the areas of thinking, language and working memory."

--2013 NYT Article

Adrianne L. Mercury

Trace the letter Aa.

A a   Animal

A A A A A A A A A

A A A A A A A A A

A A A A A A A A A

A A A A A A A A A

A A A A A A A A A

A A A A A A A A A

a a a a a a a a a a

a a a a a a a a a a

a a a a a a a a a a

a a a a a a a a a a

a a a a a a a a a a

Beginning Cursive: Alphabet Handwriting Practice

Trace the letter Aa.

A a   Analyze

A A A A A A A A

A A A A A A A A

A A A A A A A A

A A A A A A A A

A A A A A A A A

A A A A A A A A

a a a a a a a a a a

a a a a a a a a a a

a a a a a a a a a a

a a a a a a a a a a

a a a a a a a a a a

Beginning Cursive: Alphabet Handwriting Practice

Trace the letter Aa. Then write the letter Aa as many times as possible.

A a   Alphabet

Beginning Cursive: Alphabet Handwriting Practice

Write the sentence onto the lines below. Then trace and write the letters.

A was an ant

Who seldom stood still,

He made a very nice house

In the side of a hill.

A A

A A

a a a

a a a

Beginning Cursive: Alphabet Handwriting Practice

Trace the letter Bb.

B b Bubble

Trace the letter Bb.

B b Blossom

Trace the letter Bb. Then write the letter Bb as many times as possible.

Bb Baby

Beginning Cursive: Alphabet Handwriting Practice

Write the sentence onto the lines below. Then trace and write the letters.

B was a book

With a binding of blue

And pictures and stories

For me and for you.

B B B

B B B

b b b

b b b

Beginning Cursive: Alphabet Handwriting Practice

Trace the letter Cc.

10 Beginning Cursive: Alphabet Handwriting Practice

Trace the letter Cc.

Beginning Cursive: Alphabet Handwriting Practice

Trace the letter Cc. Then write the letter Cc as many times as possible.

C c Camel

Write the sentence onto the lines below. Then trace and write the letters.

C was a cat

Who ran after a rat

But his courage did fail

When she seized on his tail.

C C C

C C C

c c c

c c c

Beginning Cursive: Alphabet Handwriting Practice

Trace the letter Dd.

D d Daffodil

Beginning Cursive: Alphabet Handwriting Practice

Trace the letter Dd.

D d Destructive

Beginning Cursive: Alphabet Handwriting Practice

Trace the letter Dd. Then write the letter Dd as many times as possible.

D d   Daytime

Write the sentence onto the lines below. Then trace and write the letters.

D was a dove,

Who lived in a wood,

With such pretty soft wings,

And so gentle and good!

D D D

D D D

d d d

d d d

Beginning Cursive: Alphabet Handwriting Practice

Trace the letter Ee.

E e Excite

Trace the letter Ee.

E e Extraordinary

Beginning Cursive: Alphabet Handwriting Practice

Trace the letter Ee. Then write the letter Ee as many times as possible.

E e Excellent

Write the sentence onto the lines below. Then trace and write the letters.

E was an eagle,

Who sat on the rocks,

And looked down on the

And the far-away flocks.

E E E

E E E

e e e

e e e

Beginning Cursive: Alphabet Handwriting Practice

Trace the letter Ff.

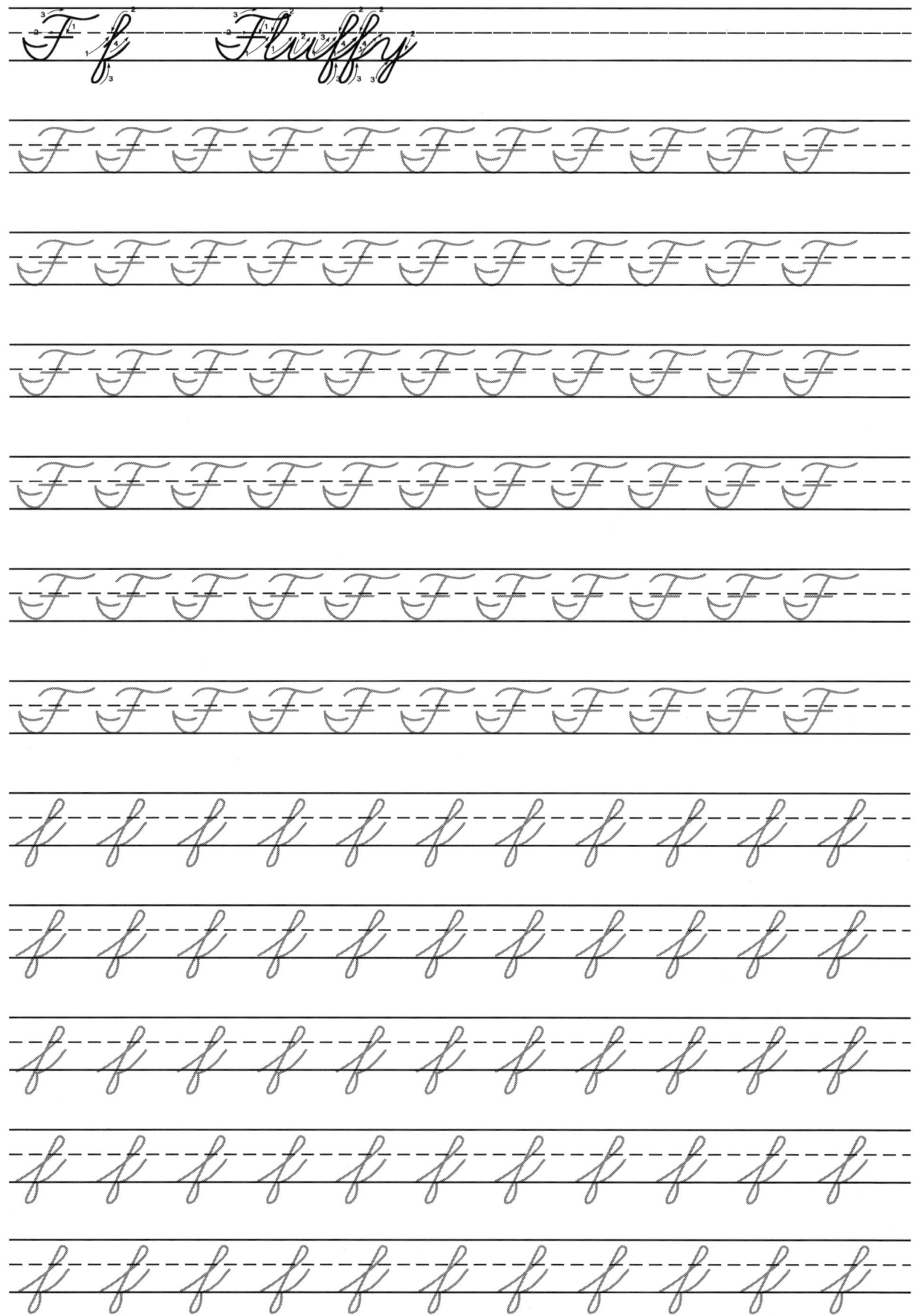

Trace the letter Ff.

Ff Flexible

Beginning Cursive: Alphabet Handwriting Practice

Trace the letter Ff. Then write the letter Ff as many times as possible.

Ff   Favorite

Write the sentence onto the lines below. Then trace and write the letters.

F was a fan

Made of beautiful stuff;

And when it was used,

It went puffy-puff-puff!

F F F

F F F

f f f

f f f

Beginning Cursive: Alphabet Handwriting Practice

Trace the letter Gg.

Trace the letter Gg.

G g Generosity

Trace the letter Gg. Then write the letter Gg as many times as possible.

G g   Gather

G G G

G G G

G G G

G G G

G G G

G G G

g g g

g g g

g g g

g g g

g g g

Beginning Cursive: Alphabet Handwriting Practice

Write the sentence onto the lines below. Then trace and write the letters.

G was a gooseberry,

Perfectly red;

To be made into jam,

And eaten with bread.

G G G

G G G

g g g

g g g

Beginning Cursive: Alphabet Handwriting Practice

Trace the letter Hh.

Hh   Heehaw

Trace the letter Hh.

H h   Hardship

Beginning Cursive: Alphabet Handwriting Practice

Trace the letter Hh. Then write the letter Hh as many times as possible.

Hh Health

Write the sentence onto the lines below. Then trace and write the letters.

H was a heron,

Who stood in a stream:

The length of his neck

And his legs was extreme.

H H H

H H H

h h h

h h h

Beginning Cursive: Alphabet Handwriting Practice

Trace the letter Ii.

Ii Insight

Trace the letter Ii.

Ii Instant

Trace the letter Ii. Then write the letter Ii as many times as possible.

Ii Itchy

Write the sentence onto the lines below. Then trace and write the letters.

I was an inkstand,

Which stood on a table,

With a pen to write with

When we are able.

l l l

l l l

i i i

i i i

Beginning Cursive: Alphabet Handwriting Practice

Trace the letter Jj.

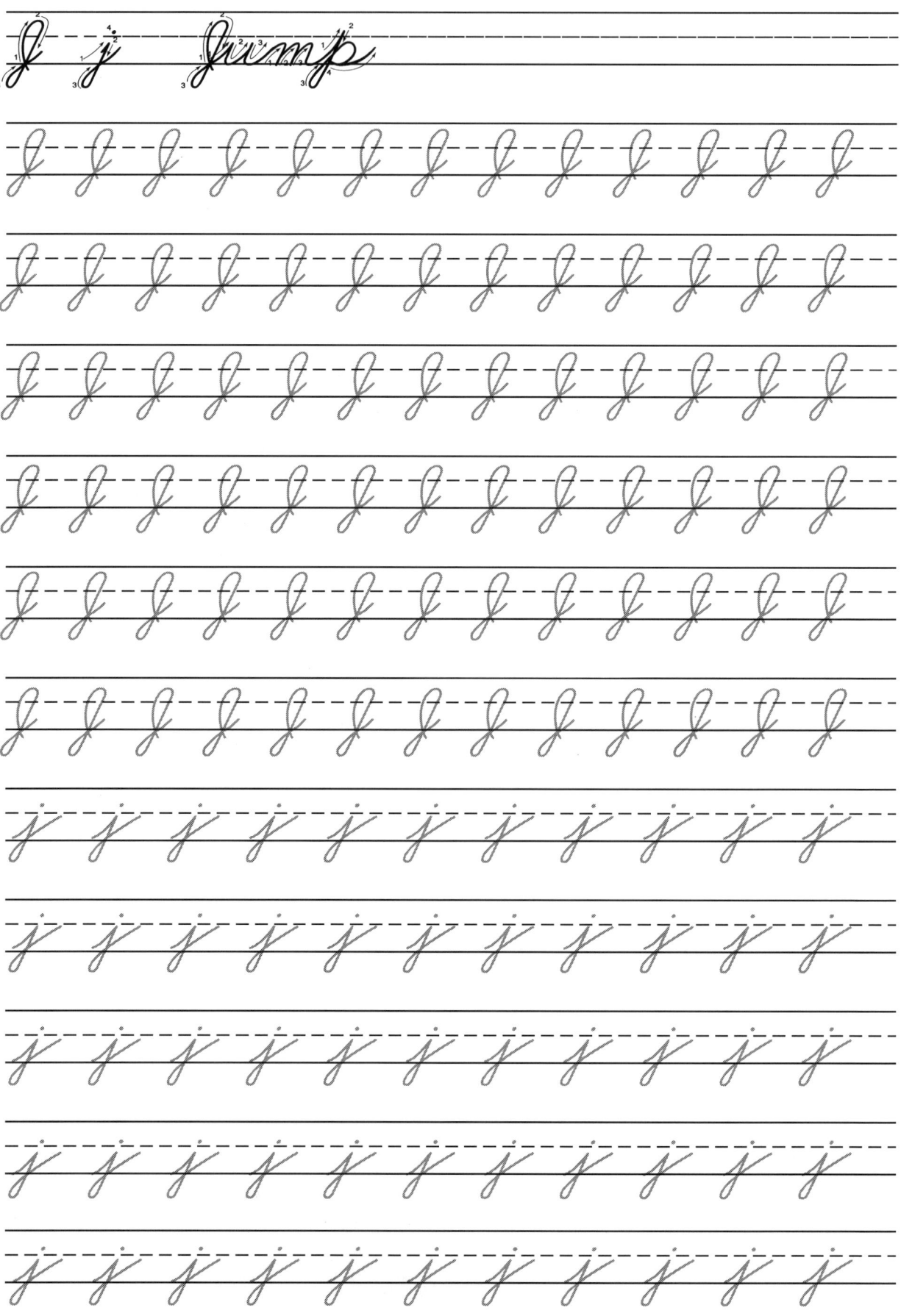

38 Beginning Cursive: Alphabet Handwriting Practice

Trace the letter Jj.

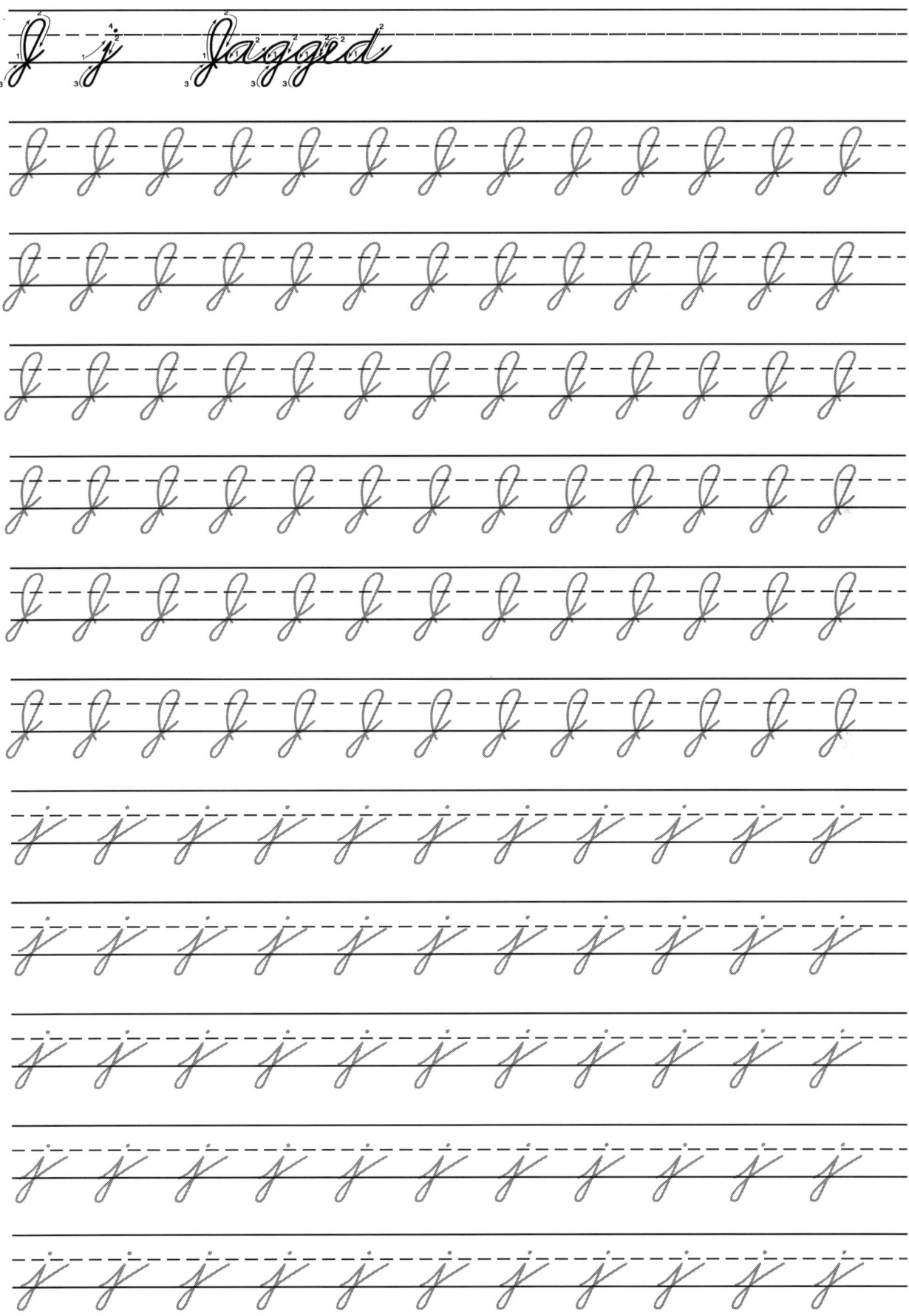

Beginning Cursive: Alphabet Handwriting Practice

Trace the letter Jj. Then write the letter Jj as many times as possible.

J j Juggle

Beginning Cursive: Alphabet Handwriting Practice

Write the sentence onto the lines below. Then trace and write the letters.

I was a jug,

So pretty and white,

With fresh water in it

At morning and night.

J J J

J J J

j j j

j j j

Trace the letter Kk.

Kk Kangaroo

Trace the letter Kk.

Kk Kinfolk

Beginning Cursive: Alphabet Handwriting Practice

Trace the letter Kk. Then write the letter Kk as many times as possible.

Kk   Karate

Write the sentence onto the lines below. Then trace and write the letters.

K was a kingfisher:

Quickly he flew,

So bright and so pretty!

Green, purple, and blue.

K K K

K K K

k k k

k k k

Beginning Cursive: Alphabet Handwriting Practice

Trace the letter Ll.

L l Lollipop

Beginning Cursive: Alphabet Handwriting Practice

Trace the letter Ll.

L l Learning

Beginning Cursive: Alphabet Handwriting Practice

Trace the letter Ll. Then write the letter Ll as many times as possible.

L l Legend

L L L

L L L

L L L

L L L

L L L

L L L

l l l

l l l

l l l

l l l

l l l

Beginning Cursive: Alphabet Handwriting Practice

Write the sentence onto the lines below. Then trace and write the letters.

L was a lily,

So white and so sweet!

To see it and smell it

Was quite a nice treat.

L L L

L L L

l l l

l l l

Beginning Cursive: Alphabet Handwriting Practice

Trace the letter Mm.

Mm Mammal

Beginning Cursive: Alphabet Handwriting Practice

Trace the letter Mm.

M m Mountain

M M M M M M M M M

M M M M M M M M M

M M M M M M M M M

M M M M M M M M M

M M M M M M M M M

M M M M M M M M M

m m m m m m m m m

m m m m m m m m m

m m m m m m m m m

m m m m m m m m m

m m m m m m m m m m

Beginning Cursive: Alphabet Handwriting Practice

Trace the letter Mm. Then write the letter Mm as many times as possible.

M m Manatee

Beginning Cursive: Alphabet Handwriting Practice

Write the sentence onto the lines below. Then trace and write the letters.

M was a man,

Who walked all around;

And he wore a long coat

That reached the ground.

M M M

M M M

m m m

m m m

Beginning Cursive: Alphabet Handwriting Practice

Trace the letter Nn.

N n Nocturnal

Trace the letter Nn.

N n Nation

Trace the letter Nn. Then write the letter Nn as many times as possible.

N n   Nanny

Beginning Cursive: Alphabet Handwriting Practice

Write the sentence onto the lines below. Then trace and write the letters.

N was a nut

So smooth and so brown!

And when it was ripe,

It fell tumble-dum-down.

N N N

N N N

n n n

n n n

Beginning Cursive: Alphabet Handwriting Practice

Trace the letter Oo.

58 Beginning Cursive: Alphabet Handwriting Practice

Trace the letter Oo.

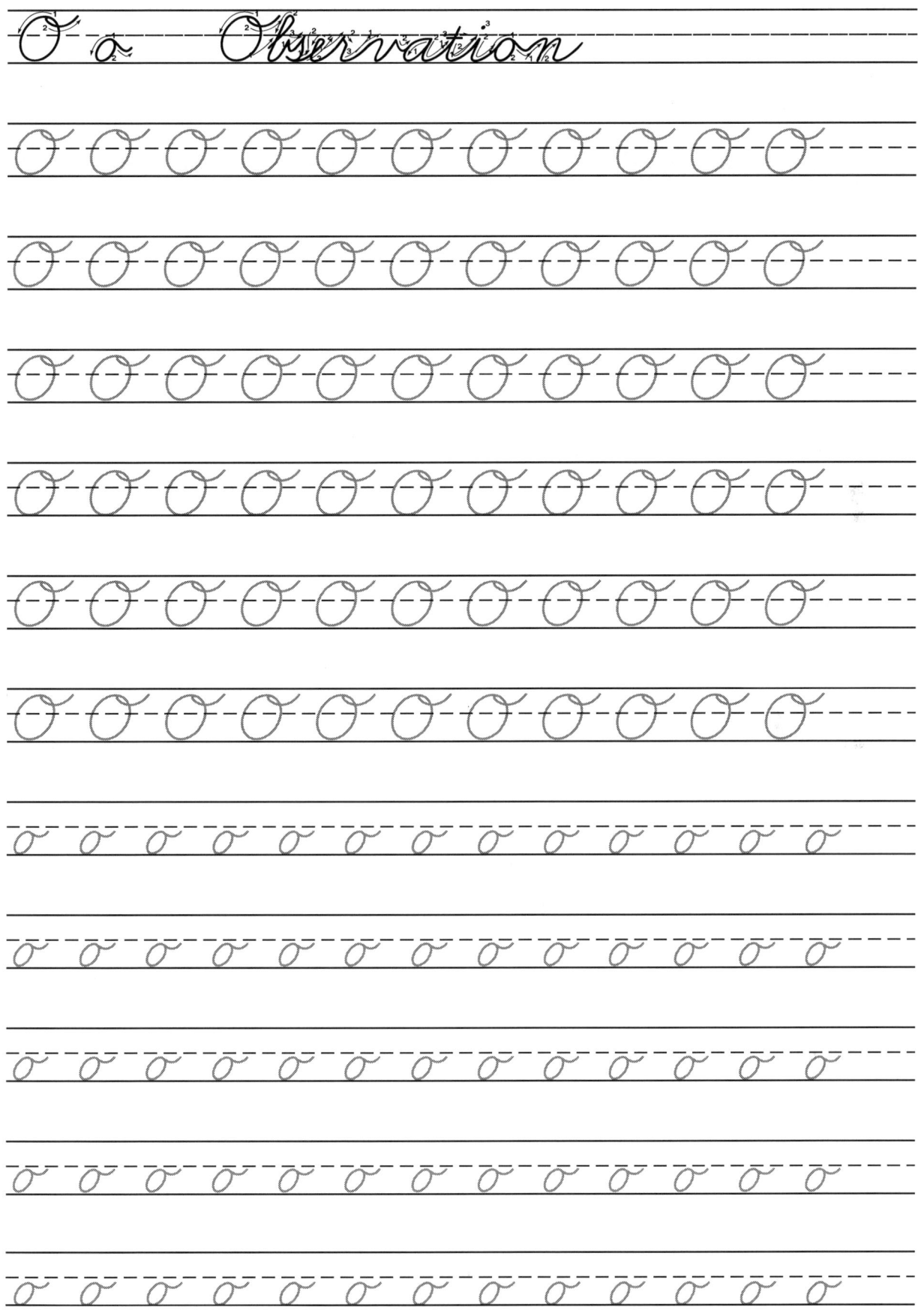

Beginning Cursive: Alphabet Handwriting Practice

Trace the letter Oo. Then write the letter Oo as many times as possible.

O o Oxygen

O O O — — —

O O O — — —

O O O — — —

O O O — — —

O O O — — —

O O O — — —

o o o — — —

o o o — — —

o o o — — —

o o o — — —

o o o — — —

Write the sentence onto the lines below. Then trace and write the letters.

O was an oyster,

Who lived in his shell:

If you let him alone,

He felt perfectly well.

O O O

O O O

o o o

o o o

Beginning Cursive: Alphabet Handwriting Practice

Trace the letter Pp.

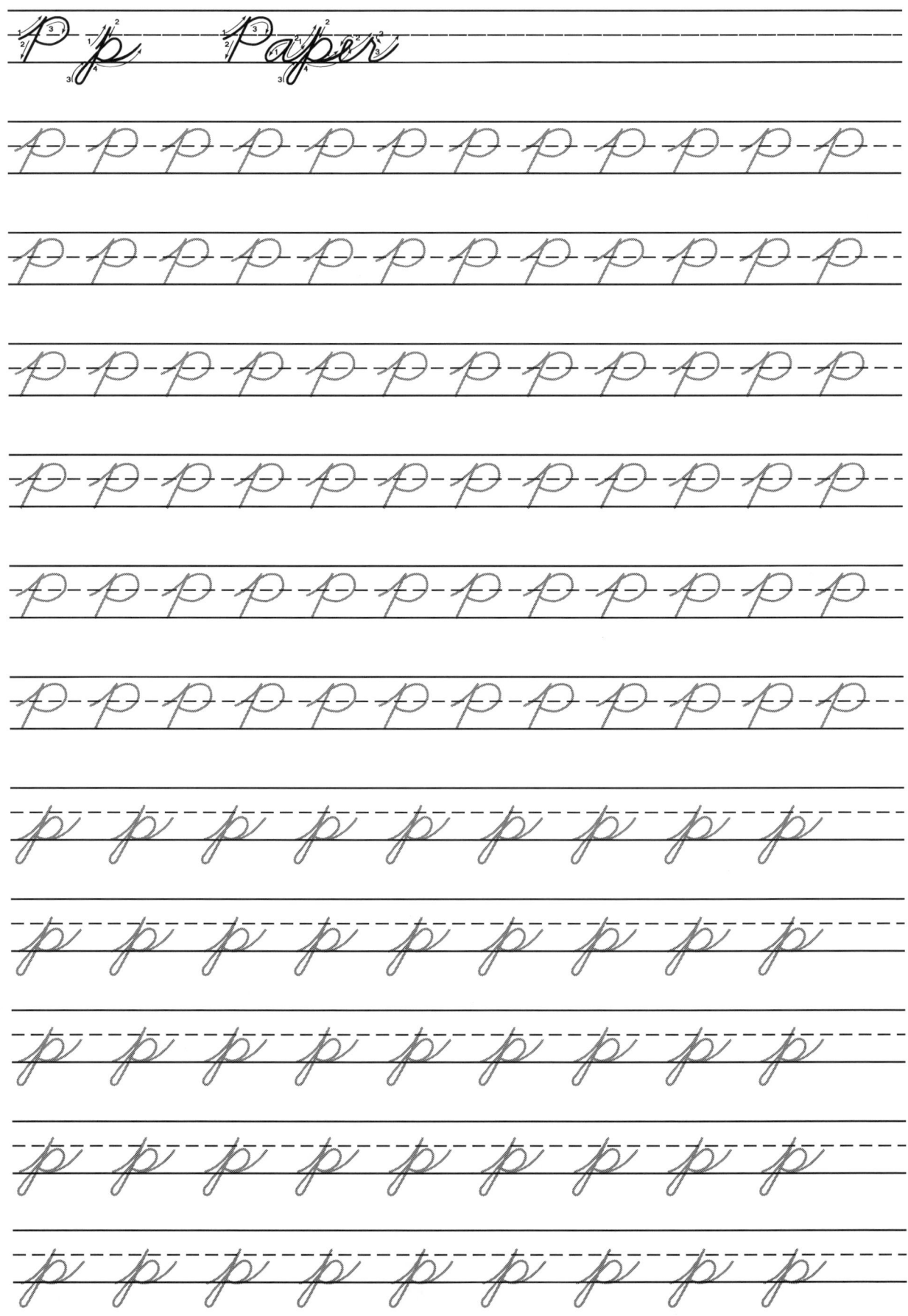

Trace the letter Pp.

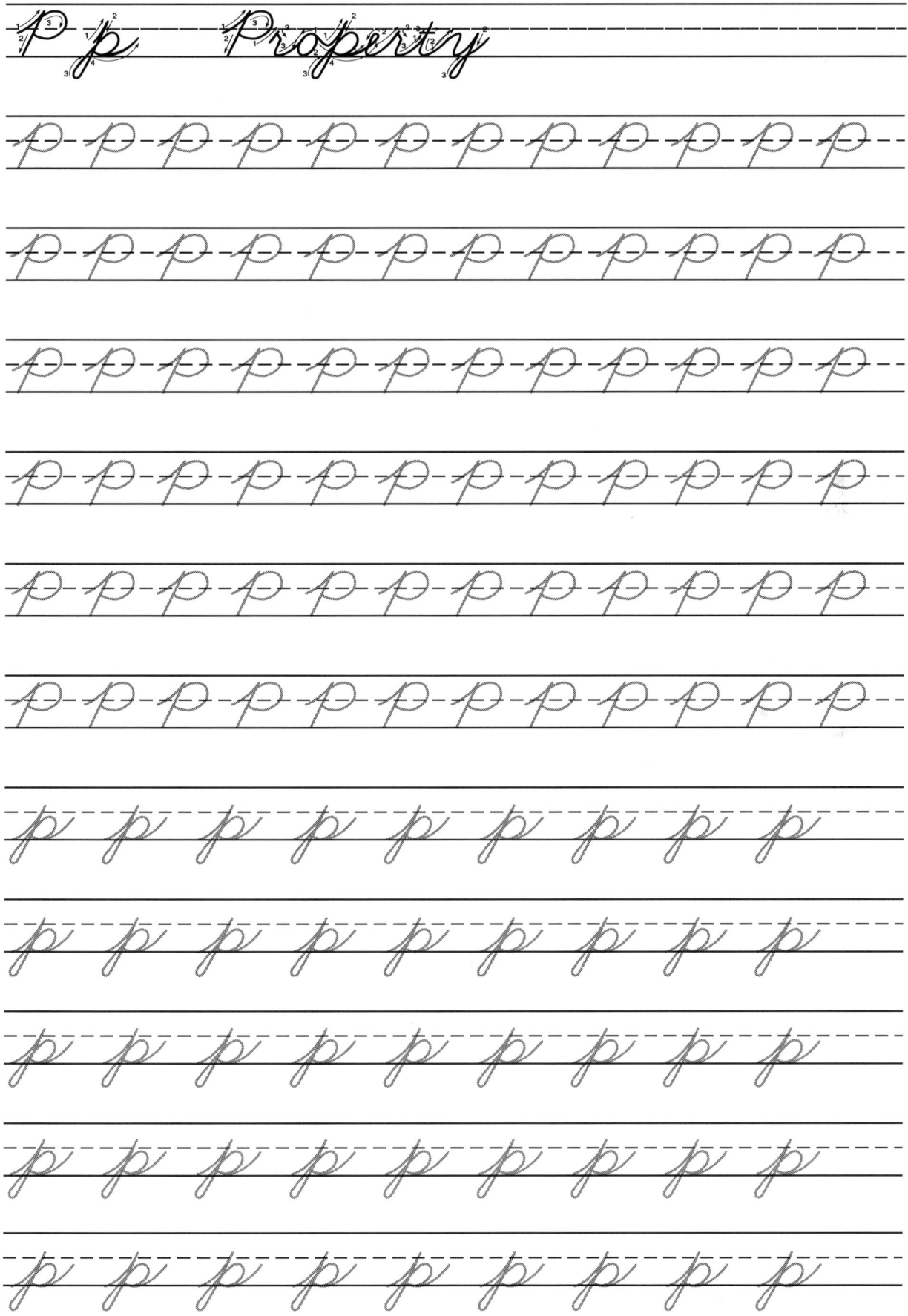

Beginning Cursive: Alphabet Handwriting Practice

Trace the letter Pp. Then write the letter Pp as many times as possible.

P p Papyrus

Beginning Cursive: Alphabet Handwriting Practice

Write the sentence onto the lines below. Then trace and write the letters.

P was a polly,

All red, blue, and green,

The most beautiful polly

That ever was seen.

P P P

P P P

p p p

p p p

Beginning Cursive: Alphabet Handwriting Practice

Trace the letter Qq.

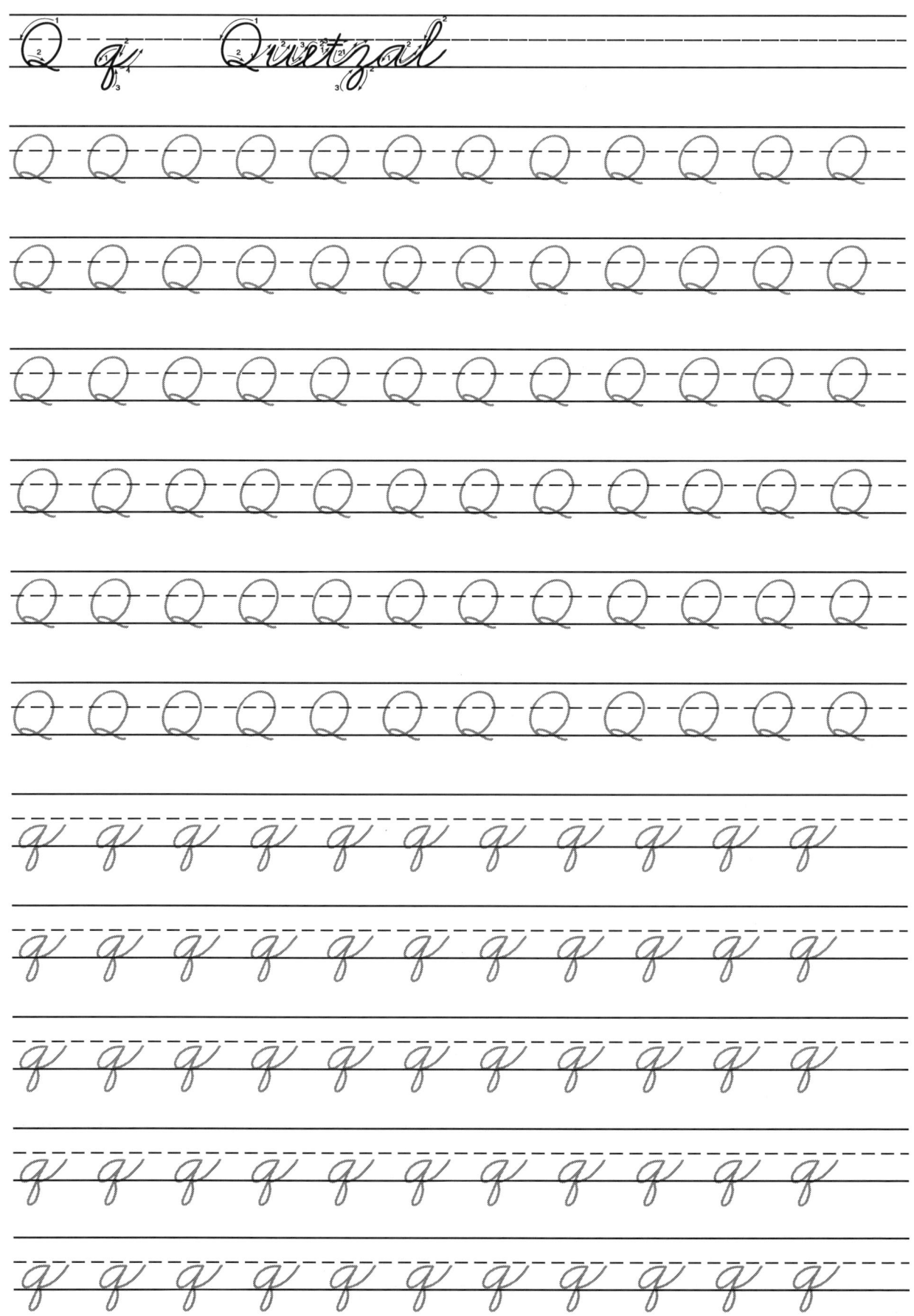

66 Beginning Cursive: Alphabet Handwriting Practice

Trace the letter Qq.

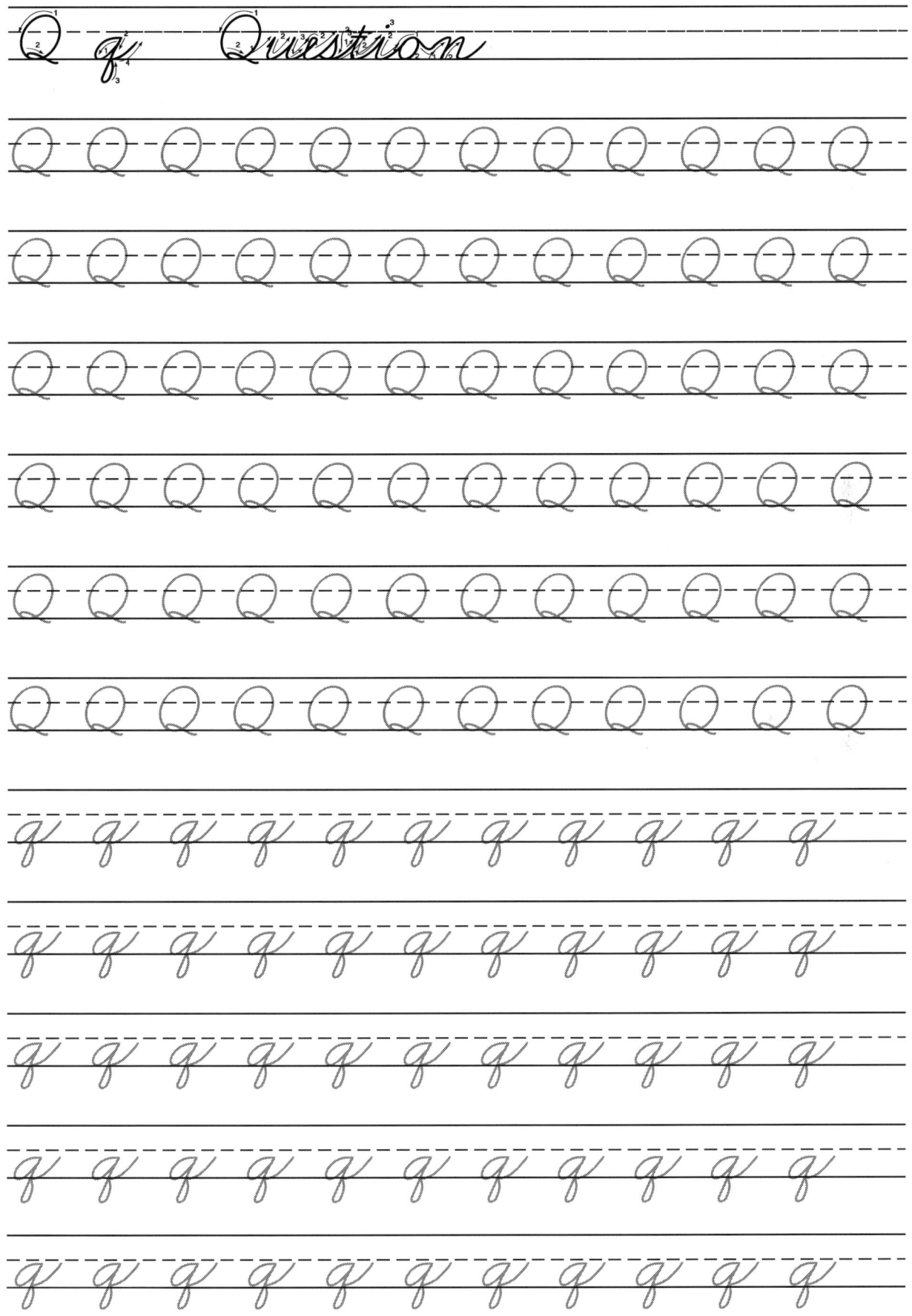

Beginning Cursive: Alphabet Handwriting Practice

Trace the letter Qq. Then write the letter Qq as many times as possible.

Q q Quaking

Beginning Cursive: Alphabet Handwriting Practice

Write the sentence onto the lines below. Then trace and write the letters.

Q was a quill

Made into a pen;

But I do not know where,

And I cannot say when.

Q Q Q

Q Q Q

q q q

q q q

Beginning Cursive: Alphabet Handwriting Practice

Trace the letter Rr.

R r Racquet

(tracing practice rows for cursive R and r)

Trace the letter Rr.

Rr Regular

Beginning Cursive: Alphabet Handwriting Practice

Trace the letter Rr. Then write the letter Rr as many times as possible.

Rr Ragweed

Beginning Cursive: Alphabet Handwriting Practice

Write the sentence onto the lines below. Then trace and write the letters.

R was a rattlesnake,

Rolled up so tight,

Those who saw him ran

For fear he should bite.

R R R

R R R

N N N

N N N

Beginning Cursive: Alphabet Handwriting Practice

Trace the letter Ss.

Ss Sunshine

Trace the letter Ss.

S s Saltfish

Beginning Cursive: Alphabet Handwriting Practice

Trace the letter Ss. Then write the letter Ss as many times as possible.

Ss Saucers

Beginning Cursive: Alphabet Handwriting Practice

Write the sentence onto the lines below. Then trace and write the letters.

S was a screw

To screw down a box;

And then it was fastened

Without any locks.

S S S

S S S

S S S

S S S

Beginning Cursive: Alphabet Handwriting Practice

Trace the letter Tt.

Tt Teapot

Beginning Cursive: Alphabet Handwriting Practice

Trace the letter Tt.

Tt Transport

Beginning Cursive: Alphabet Handwriting Practice

Trace the letter Tt. Then write the letter Tt as many times as possible.

Tt Taxicab

T T T

T T T

T T T

T T T

T T T

T T T

t t t

t t t

t t t

t t t

t t t

Write the sentence onto the lines below. Then trace and write the letters.

I was a thimble,

Of silver so bright!

When placed on the finger,

It fitted so tight!

F F F

F F F

t t t

t t t

Beginning Cursive: Alphabet Handwriting Practice

Trace the letter Uu.

Uu Unstruck

U U U U U U U U U U

U U U U U U U U U U

U U U U U U U U U U

U U U U U U U U U U

U U U U U U U U U U

U U U U U U U U U U

uu uu uu uu uu uu uu uu

uu uu uu uu uu uu uu uu

uu uu uu uu uu uu uu uu

uu uu uu uu uu uu uu uu

uu uu uu uu uu uu uu uu

Beginning Cursive: Alphabet Handwriting Practice

Trace the letter Uu.

Uu Under

Trace the letter Uu. Then write the letter Uu as many times as possible.

Uu Unwound

U U U

U U U

U U U

U U U

U U U

U U U

u u u

u u u

u u u

u u u

u u u

Write the sentence onto the lines below. Then trace and write the letters.

U was an upper-coat,

Woolly and warm,

To wear over all

In the snow or the storm.

U U U

U U U

u u u

u u u

Beginning Cursive: Alphabet Handwriting Practice

Trace the letter Vv.

Vv Valve

Trace the letter Vv.

Beginning Cursive: Alphabet Handwriting Practice 87

Trace the letter Vv. Then write the letter Vv as many times as possible.

V v   Vacuum

Write the sentence onto the lines below. Then trace and write the letters.

V was a veil

With a border upon it,

And a ribbon to tie it

All round a pink bonnet.

V V V

V V V

v v v

v v v

Trace the letter Ww.

W w   Wallow

Trace the letter Ww.

Beginning Cursive: Alphabet Handwriting Practice 91

Write the sentence onto the lines below. Then trace and write the letters.

W w Weather

W W W

W W W

W W W

W W W

W W W

W W W

w w w

w w w

w w w

w w w

w w w

Beginning Cursive: Alphabet Handwriting Practice

Trace the letter Ww. Then write the letter Ww as many times as possible.

W was a watch,

Where, in letters of gold,

The hour of the day

You might always behold.

Trace the letter Xx.

Xx Xerox

Trace the letter Xx.

X x   Xylose

Trace the letter Xx. Then write the letter Xx as many times as possible.

Xx Xanthium

Beginning Cursive: Alphabet Handwriting Practice

Write the sentence onto the lines below. Then trace and write the letters.

X was King Xerxes,

Who wore on his head

A mighty large turban,

Green, yellow, and red.

X X X

X X X

x x x

x x x

Beginning Cursive: Alphabet Handwriting Practice

Trace the letter Yy.

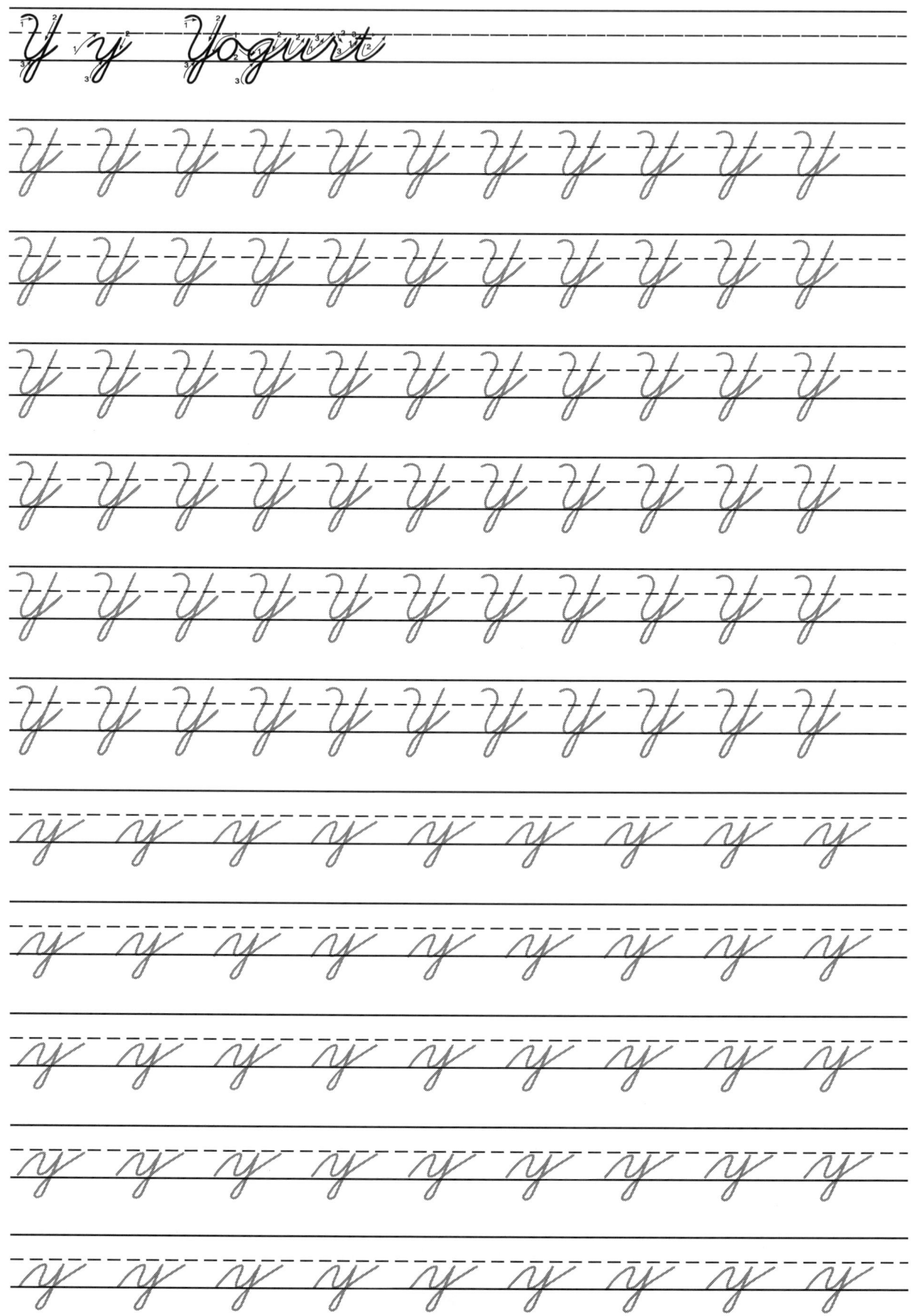

Trace the letter Yy.

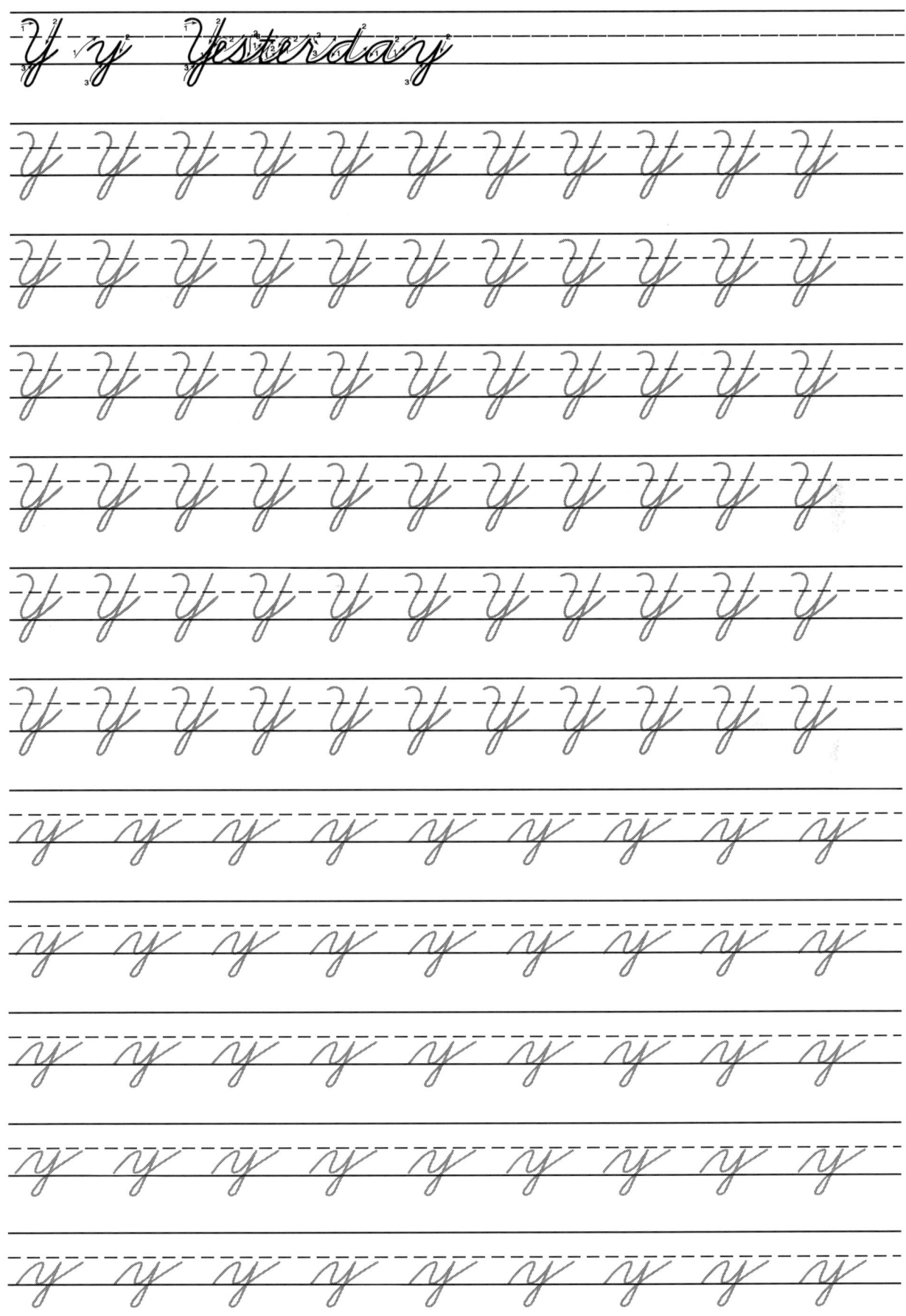

Beginning Cursive: Alphabet Handwriting Practice

Trace the letter Yy. Then write the letter Yy as many times as possible.

𝒴 𝓎   𝒴𝑒𝒶𝓈𝓉

Beginning Cursive: Alphabet Handwriting Practice

Write the sentence onto the lines below. Then trace and write the letters.

Y was a yak,

From the land of Thibet:

Except his white tail,

He was all black as jet.

Y Y Y

Y Y Y

y y y

y y y

Beginning Cursive: Alphabet Handwriting Practice

Trace the letter Zz.

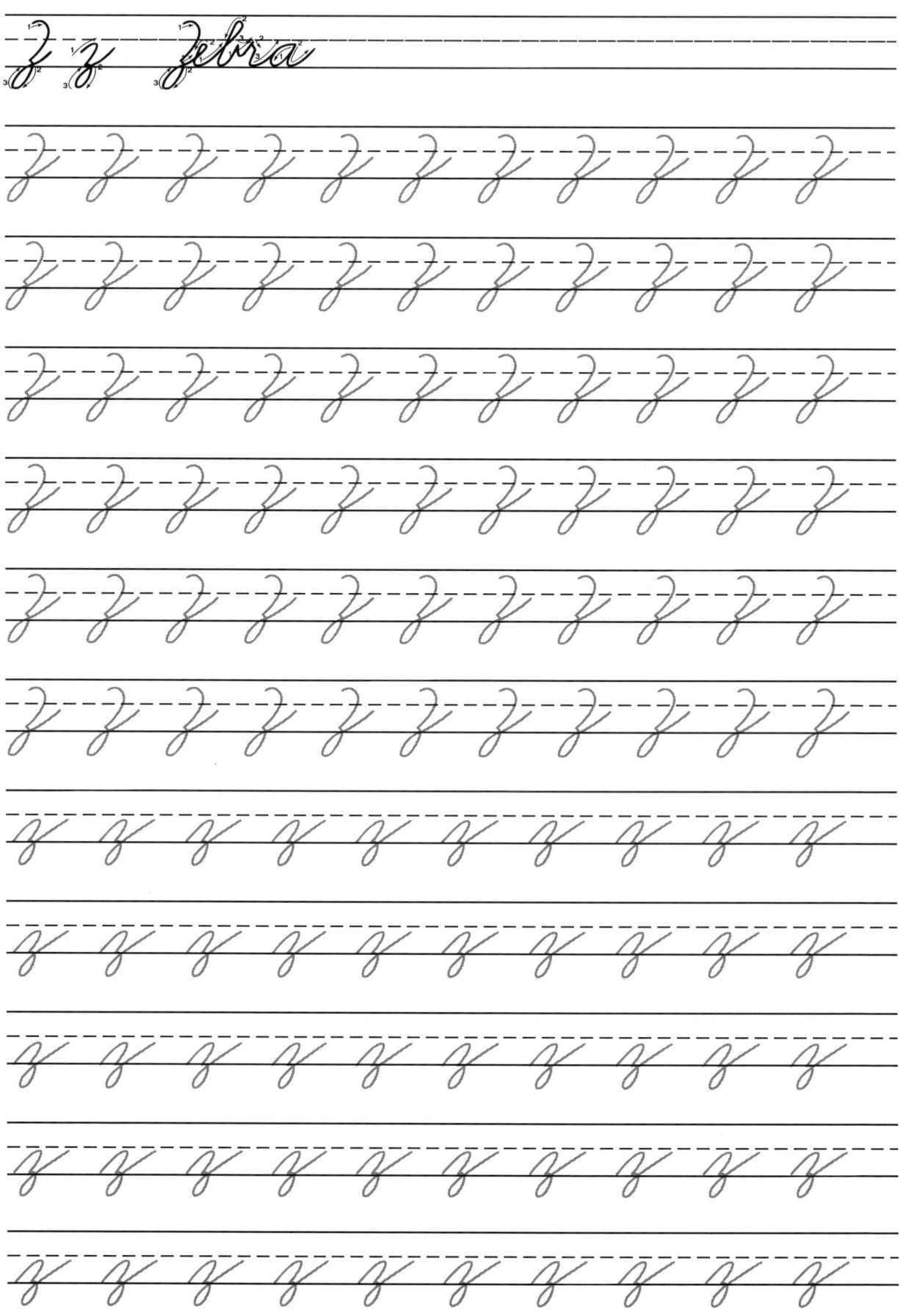

Beginning Cursive: Alphabet Handwriting Practice

Trace the letter Zz.

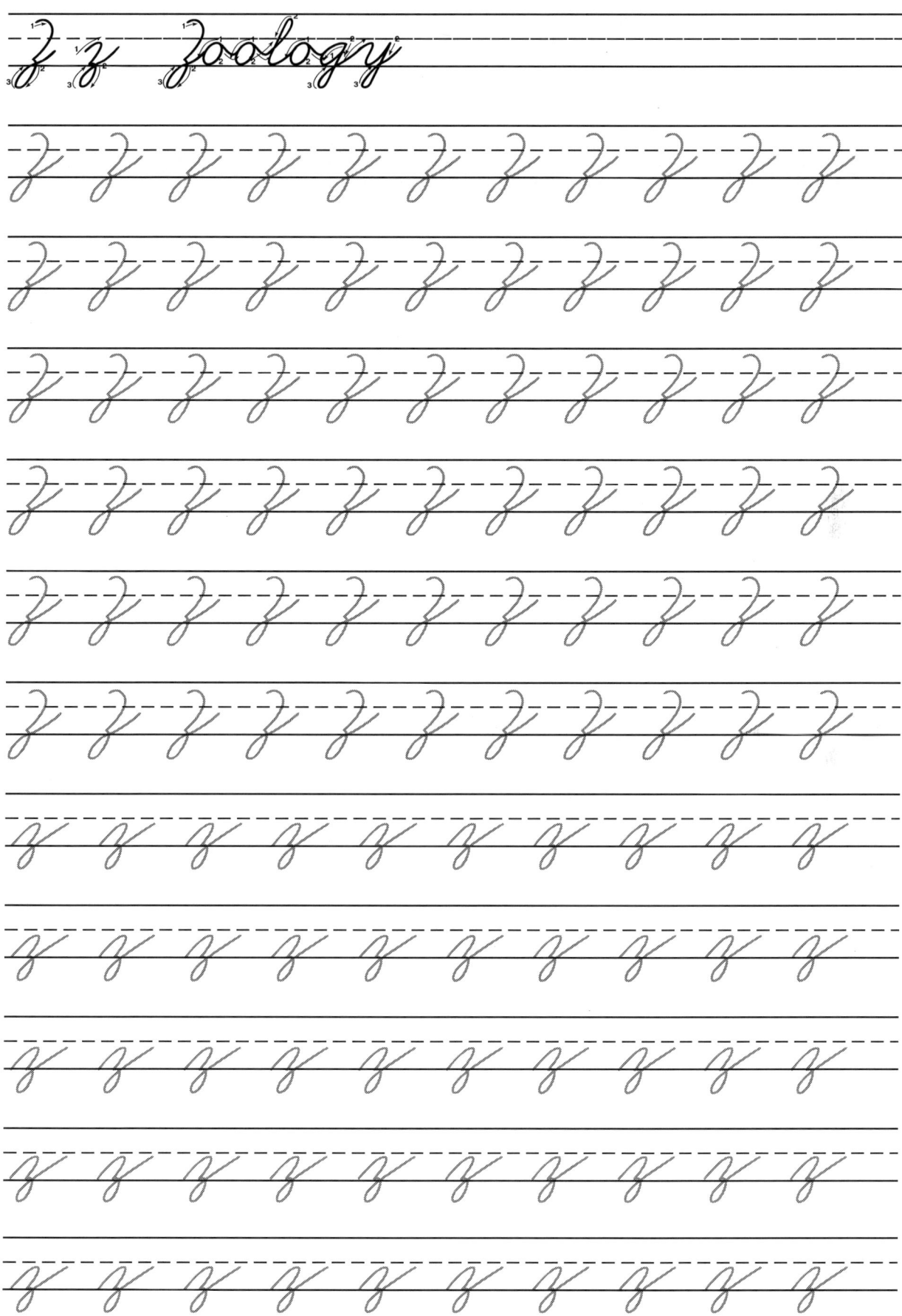

Beginning Cursive: Alphabet Handwriting Practice

Trace the letter Zz. Then write the letter Zz as many times as possible.

Zz Ziplock

Write the sentence onto the lines below. Then trace and write the letters.

Z was a zebra,

Striped white and black;

And if he were tame,

You might ride on his back.

Z Z Z

Z Z Z

z z z

z z z

Beginning Cursive: Alphabet Handwriting Practice

Printed in Great Britain
by Amazon